DEAR CARTOON LOVERS,
[and any other kind of lovers too, as far as that goes.]

There's a marvelous new school of cartooning: the Brant Parker, Johnny Hart, Bill Rechin School. The creations of these men are, without a doubt, the funniest stuff in the funnies! *

Now Parker and Rechin have spawned the great new comic strip, CROCK, and have stuffed the wonderfully off-beat characters between the covers of this here book you're holding. Great, great stuff!!

Take it from me, you too will fall down laughing,

Virgil Partch

*ACTUALLY HART, RECH̶
ARE FICTITIOUS CHAR̶

D1440224

CROCK

Drawn by Bill Rechin
Written by Don Wilder
Rewritten & Redrawn
by Brant Parker

CORONET BOOKS
Hodder Fawcett, London

Copyright © 1975, 1976, 1977 Field Enterprises, Inc.

Copyright © 1977 CBS Publications,
The Consumer Publishing Division of CBS, Inc.

First published by Fawcett Publications, Inc. 1977

Coronet edition 1979

Printed in Great Britain for Hodder
Fawcett Ltd., Mill Road, Dunton Green,
Sevenoaks, Kent (Editorial Office: 47
Bedford Square, London WC1 3DP) by
Hunt Barnard Printing Ltd.,
Aylesbury, Bucks.

ISBN 0 340 23230 7

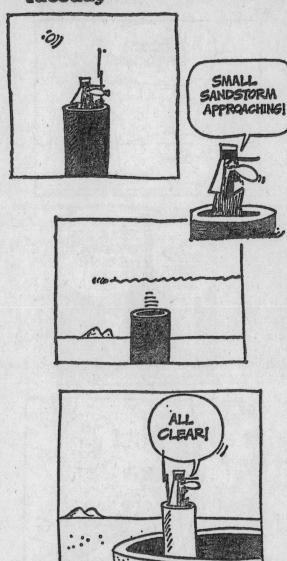

..YOU SHOULD TELL THE PRISONERS THEY DON'T HAVE TO SNAP TO ATTENTION WHEN YOU PASS, SIR...

saturday

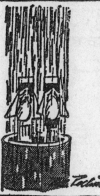

tuesday

thursday

TO HONOR THE BIRTHDAY OF THAT FAMOUS SOLDIER OF FORTUNE, PHILLIPE LABAUM..

...YOU WILL TAKE A 20-HOUR RUN WITH FULL PACKS

GAWD.. THAT'S ROUGH!

THE ROUGH PART IS BLOWING OUT THE CANDLES WHEN WE GET BACK.

Bill Rechin

tuesday

thursday

3

tuesday

thursday

HOW I ENVY YOU, LITTLE BIRD.... YOU CAN FLY TO AND FROM THOSE EXOTIC PLACES.... MARSEILLES.... SINGAPORE... BAGDAD...

BURRUP!

.... BERNIE'S PIZZA HUT...

thursday

saturday

IT'S TIME ONCE AGAIN TO SEARCH YOUR HEARTS AND GIVE GENEROUSLY TO THE "CROCK MEMORIAL FUND."

THOSE WHO GIVE WILL RECEIVE A GOLD PIN...

...AND THOSE WHO DON'T GIVE WILL RECEIVE A LARGE BRONZE PLAQUE...

...IN THE TEETH.

tuesday

thursday

thursday

tuesday

tuesday

MORE MAGIC FROM THE
WIZARD OF ID

All these books are available at your local bookshop or newsagent, or can be ordered direct from the publisher. Just tick the titles you want and fill in the form below.

Prices and availability subject to change without notice.

CORONET BOOKS, P.O. Box 11, Falmouth, Cornwall.

Please send cheque or postal order, and allow the following for postage and packing:

U.K. – One book 22p plus 10p per copy for each additional book ordered, up to a maximum of 32p.

B.F.P.O. and EIRE – 22p for the first book plus 10p per copy for the next 6 books, thereafter 4p per book.

OTHER OVERSEAS CUSTOMERS – 30p for the first book and 10p per copy for each additional book.

Name ....

Address ....

....